SECULAR GAMES

Alex Wylie's first collection interrogates and celebrates our
capacity for invention, swither, vision and delusion. Exuberant
in their range of voice and register, the poems are technically
adroit, happy to rhyme 'TV' with 'topsy-turvy' and 'Teletubby'; or
'weather' with 'whether'; elsewhere, 'lyres' metamorphose into
'liars'. Darkness lurks behind the playful language. Reality is a series
of alternatives, the toss of a coin, as adumbrated by Wylie's fine
version of Borges' *A una moneda*. Sometimes elegantly 'spinning
out a single thread further // than it should reasonably stretch',
sometimes honestly perplexed by 'a thing / you can't believe is real
/ but is', Alex Wylie has written a book for our age.
– CIARAN CARSON

Secular Games

Alex Wylie

Games

POETRY

EYEWEAR PUBLISHING

First published in 2018
by Eyewear Publishing Ltd
Suite 333, 19-21 Crawford Street
Marylebone, London W1H 1PJ
United Kingdom

Cover design and typeset by Edwin Smet
Author photograph by Joanne Dornan

Printed in England by TJ International Ltd, Padstow, Cornwall

ISBN 978-1-912477-24-1

WWW.EYEWEARPUBLISHING.COM

for Joanne

Alex Wylie was born in Blackpool in 1980.
He lived in Belfast for thirteen years, where he taught
modern literature at Queen's University Belfast, also
completing a PhD on modern and contemporary poetry.
He has published poetry in such places as *PN Review, The
Financial Times, Stand, Agenda, The Yellow Nib, Glasgow
Review of Books*, and *New Poetries V*. Wylie is also a widely-
published literary critic. He now lives in Leeds, and is a
lecturer at York St John University.

TABLE OF CONTENTS

1

2

3

The longest period of the life of man is only equal to the intermediate space between these games. For an age, or the space of one hundred years, which we call αἰών, is by the Romans called *seculum*. This is an excellent remedy for the plague, consumption and other diseases; of its origin receive this account.

Zosimus, *Nova Historia*

[I] had precisely the feeling that comes over one when the curtain goes up at amateur theatricals. Here were we, the performers, until so recently, idly sitting in the wings. There was the audience waiting to give us the reception we deserved...

Stanley Casson, *Steady Drummer*

1

PICTURES

The men with pipes and braces lean
Like cornstalks frozen in a trench.
Their pint-pots glitter, damascene;
Victoriana; serving-wench;

It's cardboard 1849
In Jarrow (not a golden year)
And workers from the local mine,
Arraigned with beer, in grainy air,

Pose to make the camera smile.
The acids of the pig-iron age
Sharpen into skin: no Sheol
Scrubbed and cleaned to make a stage –

These people were not actors. They,
Like orators of ancient Rome,
If they could speak, would, nodding, say,
The rule of law begins at home.

My friend and I discuss 'Guernica',
Goya, Edvard Munch's 'The Scream',
The church in P— where swastika
And cross are meshed and co-blaspheme

Against the wall – dear God! – the sight
Of industry from various quays –
The slant dawn-wire unpicked by light –
The new town. Furnished factories.

I turn away to drink, and rest
My flickery reflected head
Against the window: palimpsest:
Crowded bar-room; flower-bed;

And then we are outside, agreed
(And drunk) that pictures never lie.
Those flowers, like a people freed,
Would nod us to complicity.

KENSHO RIVER

Stepping across the river, Huang Po
caught himself reflected in its glass.
A white horse with black mane, upside-down,
trailed its dray; a hen corralled her chicks
into the engulfing pool of sky.

Huang Po was closer to that water
than his own image. He saw himself
awash with moss, the stream bright with cloud –
his body drawn backward from the rock
like Chicken-and-Egg, like Cart-and-Horse.

THE STAR AND THE DITCH

1
A scholar passed this way, in the dark autumn
Of tradition, lodged in the house you see –
Was commonly heard to hope for a night
Free of clouds, his haggard man unloading,
For observance of *the angels' country*.
Through glowering pipe-smoke, the folk saw him
Robed in piety and city self-regard,
A discovery of foreign linens, between
Puckered bowls of vinegar, cabbage-hearts –
But liked the sound of his coins in their brass.
Let him open his charts to the wind, if he wants,
They said. *Let him follow his comet's course,*
Pay his money, be forgotten.
Having eaten, out he went, case in hand,
His man blinking by the unstowed luggage.
As he passed, the candles shook their elfin heads.
Laughing, he would be back for the next meal.
But when hours had passed without return, they feared him robbed, or dead.

They came upon him that morning, at dawn,
His gear all bent, spun out of reach,
Frightened hands upstretching from the ditch.

2
The earth's curve is not visible from here,
This distance; you must be further away,
So the horizon can no longer be seen.
So with this moonstruck man. Year by year,
Orion's flesh developed in his eye

Like a fevered death-bed scene
Painted when he passed the test of birth.
I wonder how he shivered through his death –
Crooked as a stick in shallow water,
Chest ragged in moonlight, anti-matter
Invisible to the seraphic lens –
Making sense
Of a map of silence. Scream of a night-bird.
Do you see him, this gooseflesh shambling towards the last word?
Or, stopping, see the lamps of a flooded town
Trembling in ditch-water, and make to touch,
Sleeves rolled to the elbows, forearms wet,
The pith of what you can't quite yet make out:
Branches raised, defying the starry ditch.

THE WRECK OF THE *CORMORANT*, 1929

No-one
could touch him after that
for loneliness. On Pharos Street
he leaned against the locked beacon, smoking
like a real ghost in the puddles' lights; kept pepped
with stringent tonics of the day – shaggy flocks of Woodbine-smoke,
the sea-embittered air – he was, but if he was, then maybe he was not
the puddle of our thoughts we thought he was, the world
like water swashing round a buckled hulk
its tides of black and white, a thing
you can't believe is real,
but is.

ITALY

Grotesques
parade along the Corso dei Servi: the poor
proceed in the grand manner, arabesques
on vestibule and dome and painted door
like scribes with spotted fingers squirming from their desks

in some eastward-facing portrait
of Milanese St Carlo, his pared-back estate,

the air
filled with satellites and fast news
of banners, salvaged victories; and, there,
the wheyfaces, the grand half-nudes
draped in Tyrian purple, blacks and violent blues:
the Cardinal's works, renounced and most rare.

UNPARABLES

The essence of discourse is prayer.

– Emmanuel Levinas

1

The Venus Lander

Thirty-five million miles of nothingness
to go, five million gone, I dream in darkness
of your skies, your sulphur, wings spread to address

the sun; balanced, for a time, in space
great minds have wandered behind screwed-up eyes,
or theorised as heaven, or dreamed of monsters

gnawing the bones of heaven as they fell.
Each day transmits me further – mechanical
half-dinosaur – closer, closer to the unreal

I was made for. And if expiry is rebirth
when the brain has burned out, and I am myth,
I will solve, forever, the riddles of your earth.

2
Judas

St Swithin's Day,
you kissed me on the cheek
I'd turned
to the luxury of sunbathers
gaggling there to see
if I would vanish
in a puff of holy smoke.
O Adonai,
I vanished in a trice –
root now among the skulls
of that many-headed beast,
a torrid pulse:
discretion's soul,
so good they damned him twice.

And on the wall
to the hibiscus kingdom
stood a sign
sprayed up by some benign
malingerer
(no doubt)
by now long gone
beyond the far gates with their nodding plumes of sun;
while I, small soul,
orbited the halo of your head –
my one fiducial point –
not god, not man, not bird
nor beast nor plant
IF U CAN READ THIS YOUR ALREADY DEAD

my blood inflaming at your pulse,
my pulse your blood
and thunder
bringing on cold sweats of rain
at noon
as shadows branched across your face.
The paths are straight
(I'm told)
on which we meet,
we whistlers in the dark,
the ones we will forsake.
Now, open your unearthly eyes and start –
as though a smoke of heaven
puffed against your cheek.

3

Rooms

Two prisoners whose cells adjoin communicate by knocking on the wall.
– Simone Weil

I
When glutted Storm
rolls redly off
Sun
rain-strutted
cloud-gravid
spatters spectral
gouts of shade
against this wall

2
You are next-door
in the lazaretto of yourself
and I receive
your lost rent
squall
of love
and

3
who
are you singing to
behind the membrane,
a wall
thin as Samhain veils,
a robin's wing

4
wispy, worn
to nothing
on a silken flux
a wind
to drive a woman mad,
skittering my sight,
the madman's wisp

5
but no
not singing –
you cry
harsh vowel-
music
trembling the purdah
of our lives
with manic breath

6
announce the god
of love
the love
of god
like an abandoned
workhouse
cat

7
at your body's
pitted arch
your cry

in cloud-light
blood
hacked into the wind

8
cigarette smoke
stippled
at the dark ionosphere
of ceiling
prison escalades
come worming out
of Piranesi's brain

9
— I came to
on the stairs,
once,
us shaking hands,
you asking
if we'd met
or was I you —

10
monarch
of the dream
and subject
to its working
you cry
Republic!
and awake
in chains

SOLILOQUY

whether
it's love or fear
brings me to you I know
I'll never make your face my own

REVISITING THE FORGE

They've given us a clue: the sound
of hammers clanging into anvils is an echo
of angelic harmony. I heard this on the radio.
According to the experts, around
520 BC a scientist
hesitated by a smithy door – slumming
it like a king in furs –
at a moment of personal crisis
impossible music, spirit's blood-beat, drumming
through the soundholes of his ears

(meanwhile the nameless blacksmith hears
a scraping at the door, looks up and hits his thumb
and screams blue murder; Pythagoras, struck dumb
in sunlight, invents the music of the spheres).

A BAROQUE CEILING

(Rubens, Whitehall Banqueting House)

They had it all, those rampant cavaliers
Brought out of limbo back to English life,

And knew it all too well; whose art proclaims
The age in redolence of sex and war,

In superhuman marble and in ceilings
Covering the white earth with skies of louche.

History a pageant, the mind its own place
As here, on high, two women struggle

In symbolic lust – one beautiful, the other foul
To look on, the one trampling the other

In the artist's vision of servility –
Avarice and Bounty, bare-armed for war,

Tumbling forever into England.

TAP-WATER

First among commodities, tap-water, drink
   Of equals, council-juice or aqua gratis;
   Cloud-confession wrung in kitchen sink
Keeping the house afloat through choppy waters;
Morning-after-wine; cat's whiskers, dog-poteen;
   Christ harrowing the waterworks of Hell
   As iron hydroxide, fluoride, chlorine;
Stream of consciousness; bottomless well;
Angel in the house, earth's better half
   Restrained in ropes of glass; oil of beggars;
   Currency, possessed of nothing but itself,
Diamonds tumbling liquid through the fingers,
Stranger, friend or enemy, O! Ingest
   The glorified remains of the Wicked Witch of the West.

FOUR VERSIONS OF BORGES

Dar y recibir son lo mismo.

– Jorge Luis Borges 1899-1986

I

Yo

The skull unseen, the heart invisible,
the motorways and byways of the blood
I cannot fix, inconstant as the god
Proteus, all nerves, guts, bones; as physical

as change itself, I am these things. And yet –
I am, too, the memory of a scimitar
slicing down the sun, and a blood-red sunset
turning grey, and darkening, and a single cellular star.

Lookout on the world's shore, I see the ships
endlessly replanked. I am the numbered books
and letters thin with time, the dry codex,
words mouthed indecently by long-dead lips.

Stranger, even, are these words I write
in a room somewhere, full of dust and light.

II

Alexander Selkirk

I dream the sea, that infinite sea... a sea
that scatters, nightmarish, at the ringing
of the bells. They sanctify the morning
of England, deep and intimate, wind-heavy.

Five years I wasted there, ignored by stars,
mithered by my shadow. Like human history
in a made-up language, I tell this story
obsessively, to strangers, in the pubs and bars.

The good Lord delivered me from that land of dream-terrors
to myself, my own house, the difficult mirrors.

Surrounded like an isle of solitude
by sea. Crowd-pleaser, with a captive stare,
why find the words to tell that crowd
the truth, that home is neither here nor there?

III

A una moneda

Sailing from Montevideo
on wintry seas, wind-heckled,
freezing round the headlands of night,
I threw a coin
from boredom and for luck.

Spinning through blackness in a heart's turn —
royal-headed silver spark
devoured
by darkness visible it seemed
to meet halfway.

I felt indelible,
forking the road
of almost-endlessness
that is the planet's history,
the doer of the un-undoable:

my own life, full of fear and love,
and then the coin's
drifting on 'til world's end
or soothed into quietus by the sea
with Saxon treasures, Viking spoils.

Dreaming or awake I see the coin,
heads-up, watchful,
suddenly ancient like a blinded eye
in darkness. I know of course
it sees me too —

but when I look at you
down the darkening fathoms of the years,
you are as lost and innocent
of time's unresting maze
as time itself.

IV
El sueño

When night's unstoppable machines
are grinding up
their raw material
I'll go
further even than Odysseus
to seas where fish are sinuous
as dreams and silvery
against the memory

and jungle-cities in the sea
cacophonous with birds
weird
shouting-matches with the dead
in words
as old as DNA

and faces fixed like death
and terror of the truth
beneath

I will be all and none –

I'll be the one
I always am
who gazes on the dream
of waking life and judges me
smiling, resigned,
even happy.

JERICHO

Funnily enough there's only air
between us, no wall
of monumental moment and renown
to storm at, blow up or bulldoze down,
nor lock to twist off with the minor key of song;

though for some reason – as you mark well –
I've brought along
my own wall-flattering trumpet to blow
with one desire, to enter Jericho.

FATHER OF LIES

The devil wants a word in private. He'll
whisper to you sweet anecdotes of hell

so you want that cliché of the dream
being real and things being just as they seem

to be just that. He'll speak from the abyss
behind the mirror – which doesn't exist,

by the way – of incorruptibles
playing with fire, frozen, hell's tables

tempting as an asbestos factory.
With mime, with methodistical ventriloquy

he'll mouth his tales of fact,
throwing in for luck the odd sound effect –

a fart, a belch, a diminishment of whale-
song. He'll want you to memorise his tales

(such tales): that she's going to leave you;
that when you speak no fucker'll believe you;

that your best friends bully you in their sleep
(your nightmares climaxed with a slap);

that your parents find your constant harassment
for affirmation an embarrassment;

that your most sainted lover
craves the impossible cock of Lucifer

in her dreams, which are real as you and me;
that all of human history's

an iron cage to house the moment of truth
in which you stand, brushing your teeth

like a god; that he's escaped from hell to get you, which he hasn't.
That he exists; which he doesn't.

FIREFLY

Come and go, my lampyrida,
Wake me with a lightbulb moment,
Phosphorescent immolation,

Visited on human beings
Ageing by degrees your parsecs,
Fragile to the zillionth power;

Come and speak your undiscovered
Dialect of body language,
Untranslatable as music,

Played in heat, on skin and cotton,
Blown by anxious ariettas
Here from there, wherever there is;

Anonymity of darkness
Compromised by morning's X-ray,
Radiant and radiating;

Ghostly fingerprints on windows,
Double-glazed and insulated.
Come and go, as distant traffic

Rumbles in the listening memory,
Out of sight, but not of earshot,
Thunder limping after lightning,

Lucifers and Roman candles,
Fairytale-apocalyptic
Words from childhood lit in fireworks,

Scribbling figure eights and zeroes
On imagination's blackboard,
Duffle-coated in the driveway,

Searing alphabetic nonsense
Winter darkness makes the most of,
Bonfires on November beaches

Spook the donkeys. Hibernation;
Consciousness; the smell of sulphur,
Bringing, as I see it, out of

Darkness bioluminescence,
Sleepless as the zeitgeist, zigzags
Fleeting as success, or money.

Adulthood, its basic future,
Melts from you like polar icecaps,
Climbs the glass like rising water

Copper-sulphate-blue aurora
Bringing you, the body's pilgrim,
Into this forsaken climate,

Wide uncomprehending doorways,
Coming, going, singing, dancing
Naked at my empty window,

Till the daylight overcomes you.

THE ISLE OF MAN

Anything for a quiet life,
now the years of slogged retreat are over,
your own little corner
of the universe to live
and die in, as you say;
a natural reserve,
tame wildlife,
keeping itself to itself;
the wind a bad connection with the sea.
The spoils of peace:
bare living quarters,
books and pots, a white
feather on a wooden foldaway
from anywhere, perhaps,
as likely Wonderland as Newfoundland,
America. Every day
it goes down like a dream. Every day
it tickles like that feather
wafted inland
from the infinite,
the world-interpreting sea,
or further, out of any
of the round earth's imagined corners
to your own.

And no, you'd never think
about the Isle of Man,
fifty miles away and less,
that cushy demolition job
you went to at seventeen,
returning three months later, hardly touched;

because we know it isn't much,
and you never were
the castaway
of grinning, pigeon-chested British sailors...
More an island, entire of itself,
as the saying goes.
Sod this for a game of soldiers.

THE AGE OF AUSTERITY

Remember when you played the golden boy?
And suddenly the news is relevant.

This time it's actually goodbye.
She's dropped you: Operation Dumbo Drop,
a parachuted elephant
rescued from the war, killed by friendly fire...

Remember? When you thought you could lever
the Milky Way into position
with your back braced against Hale-Bopp,
immortally clever
strongman and metaphysician?

Now you can't get interviewed, never mind hired.
In the red not the pink.

A fat fiddling statue, if golden you were, that belly-
flopped
into the world's
alkaline puddle, all your glistering gold
washed up to wafer-thin paint and alloy.

Don't you ever think,
perhaps you never were the golden boy –
that when everybody feted you,
loved you, in actual fact, they hated you?

PLEASURE BOATS

The pleasure boats have got away to sea,
Queen of England, Boadicea, Lady of the Lakes,
shed their instincts
for mooring
like ropes, for reasons indistinct,
the tour-guides witless on the jetty,
coastguard past calling.

How they even got there is a mystery
profound beyond measure,
unfathomable, as horses out of their depth
buck the swell
carrying no rider.
Off-peak,
the pleasure boats are nowhere to their pleasure.

Rain hovers on the sea, like...
Whatever happens, we'll never know,
till the weather
break,
what's salvaged – if
petrified recoveries of horn and hoof,
or whether
Queen of England, Boadicea, Lady of the Lakes.

MYSTERIES

I remember inventing mysteries
one summer in the back yard with my sister;
hiding in the flower-bed, and the bird-watch
for that face out of nightmare, of the witch

who squatted in the empty bungalow,
appearing (horror!) in the criss-cross window.
(My sister saw it when she closed her eyes –
that's how she knew she'd got the same disease,

she said. I said I thought I had it too.)
Improvising storylines illogical
as Genesis, and her a stickler
for making the improvised come out as true,

occasionally we'd outdo ourselves:
like the time I found the bloody garden gloves
in the middle of one mystery's momentum,
cold water to the dream, its twisted arm,

fingering the unknown murderer
too soon. The plot could go no further.
She closed the case. We went inside for tea.
But, since every good detective team

functions, malfunctions, as a double act,
one stolid, the other mentally wrecked,
as she washed her hands for tea, I pretended
to be the killer, uncaught, red-handed,

tiptoeing my deviance alone
in the calm, quick knowledge it was me all along.
I've always known the murderer's identity.
Now she's a sometime revolutionary

in Buenos Aires, Argentina, far
as can be from that over-the-shoulder fear –
and every day, since I was sane and small,
I see the killer's smiling face, and smile.

A BOX OF DARKNESS

I brought you a box of darkness
for your going away
from which the cat had long escaped
into the world of light,
leaving the darkness behind
inside the box.

The lid being shut
you couldn't see what wasn't
or was alive
inside, or dip your hand
for the puny fish-bite of fangs
that wouldn't come,
in the dark in the light.

Once opened, like cloudy water
darkness
light-polluted
lapped at the brim, the well
that had swallowed the cat
or it escaped,
padding pawprints of darkness
like invisible ink

and this much now you knew:
that my gift for your going away
was a box
a box of darkness
plonked down in the middle of a swirling room
of dark
energy and puzzling dimensions.

So, where's my present then?

Good question.
Follow the pawprints of invisible ink
I didn't say, nor
it's a thought experiment
– or open the curtains
onto a day
weird as a new universe
infinite with cats
escaping
everywhere and nowhere,
in the dark in the light.

THE SILKWORM CHAMBER

But I remember that I am no more than a mutilated being who
dwells in degradation. Anything I might attempt to do would meet
with censure.
– Sima Qian, letter to Ren An

Standing before you of my own free will
this doesn't mean I'm here to fulfil

a promise to my dying father
to be the one and only honest writer

of history, so to speak, to compare
with the back-breaking conscience of an empire

batted back and forth from palm to palm
as cocoons of the Asiatic silkworm

are ferreted out, weighed and checked
for quality, the brittle intellect

fondled in the operative's fingers
for density of fibres

reeled through the machine,
translucent, like a film of crepe de chine

– and yes, unrolling the metaphor –
in ribbons on the cutting-room floor

a history spun into a yarn
to clothe an emperor and strike his yen

for eunuchs made celebrities by this,
quote unquote, punishment of rottenness

taking their liberal pinch of salt
like a final insult

rubbed into the wound
stand back as it's efficiently wound

with airy swathes of habotai,
and do not suture up the cavity.

Nor am I not losing my mind
but losing everything except my mind

or more than my last remaining nerve
though disingenuously naïve

speaking humbly of my own free will
and not, repeat, not, here to fulfil

a promise to my dying father,
spinning out a single thread further

than it should reasonably stretch,
stitching more than it should seem to stitch,

as expert on the ancient kings of Qin
as I am about the hereto-unnamed Sima Qian.

(Always take out more than you leave in,
they say: a principle for living,

not dying, by. I make no living
by these, er, private parts I do leave in.)

And so on. Better late than never
to mention the equivocal survivor

of the tale, not executed with aplomb,
a living/preserved exemplum,

resigning his *privy member*
for life's recuperation in the Silkworm Chamber,

proving, after all efforts to perempt,
that sometimes you don't die in the attempt.

PROPAGANDA

WHAT'S MEANT FOR YOU WON'T PASS YOU BY
the poster in the union grins
at me, and other passers-by
who may or may not pass it by
unseeing it, as I see it,

apparently not meant for those
who pass it by. I see it, though;
altruistic fateful clang
in letters white as teeth, a type
as bold as brass, as true as hype:

what's meant for you is meaningful
(*you* being me, and also you).
What's meant for you will pass you by
if it wasn't meant for you:
the axiom is circular.

It eats itself, with teeth as white
as Californian basking sharks'
who turn upon themselves and tear
at their own bleeding tails, as white
as toothpaste and Pacific spume,

it eats itself – spits toothpaste out,
Pacific spume. What's meant for me
has passed me by, will pass me by,
and what I mean may pass you by,
and you may pass by what I mean.

2

A NOVELIST CAN'T FINISH HER DEBUT NOVEL

1: GAZA

A novelist in terror of her characters
coming to life and dying again in Ramallah

under a plague of rockets from Tel-Aviv
can't finish her book. Cutting-edge TV

in which the Channel 4 News
is like a nightly accusation of abuse

destroys her; information; abstract concretes;
funeral riots in the narrow streets,

ginnels of the international city;
the over-complication of complicity...

There is no current situation in her book.
In other news, General Mubarak

said that today's peace talks have been hijacked.
If the first casualty of war is fact

its final arbiter is fiction.
She fears she is the idol of a faction.

Children are gripping, unputdownable
as Friedrich de la Motte Fouqué's *Undine*.

Maybe you don't know it. And Israel
battles the angel in the fairy-tale

from the year dot, a Huldebrand
who sallies forth into a forbidding land

and finds his children, who worship someone else,
to whom they cry aloud and cut themselves.

2: UKRAINE

A novelist repenting of her plotline
sees her fingerprints all over east Ukraine,

snowglobes, doorhandles, the Orthodox
Christ; Kiev, Sevastopol, Donetsk,

blown into globs of crimson Russian glass:
in the spirit of absolute glasnost

her fingerprints abound, for all the world
hurricane blueprints, glowering cloud-whorls

squeezing the monochrome steppes of Kansas,
Dorothy ravening there, behind, on all fours.

She'd rather be a demon than a journalist.
Being, however, a 'magical realist',

she's neither and both; her darlings
are loyal to her godhead as the Higgs

boson is in love with Professor Peter
Higgs; i.e. get real: they're characters

written by themselves, scatty ciphers,
suffering as *The Last Unicorn* suffers –

and nothing more. No life to anything,
and no death, either. Vladimir Putin

explains, again, how the modern state works,
Imperial-Oligarchic-Orthodox,

on state TV; commemorates Chernobyl.
She's nearly finished her englobing novel.

3: BELFAST

A novelist in love with the idea
of falling in love with this very idea

squints up at the bold **VIVA PALESTINE**
in white letters high on Black Mountain

and, crossing the road, falls in a hole instead,
stretches to infinite length at infinite speed,

popping out, yesterday, in a parallel
reality. **AVIV ISRAEL**

in black letters high on White Mountain
(spring harvests, the green shoots of autumn)

wealth distributed according to worth;
Irish fishing trawlers docked at Portsmouth,

a bawn of masts; films about cameramen;
Falls Road murals of David Cameron,

crowned with laurels, with hawk-eyed sceptre,
Imperator of the Public Sector.

She hates this story: a world fine-tuned
to the whimsy of an omnipotent mind

on an off-day. Curious, isn't it,
she muses – how the very word *zenith*

is one scribe's misreading of the Arabic
and man's eye view of planetary ecliptic...

She wakes on a park bench by the Lagan,
out of sight, and mind, of **PALESTINE,**

and, in the singularity of her idea,
rises in celebration of *nadir*.

4: IRAQ

A novelist in dread of her own postscript
being nasty, brutish, and abrupt,

won't write it. Yet. Yet, what's an epilogue
if not a post-traumatic prologue,

a final breakdown of means into end?
To write an ending one flooded weekend

a century after the First World War
kicked off in France. Or Belgium. Or somewhere.

The bulk of the novel's long-since-written
but never ended, begun, or yet forgotten.

Like a meditation on *jihad*.
Whether suicide bombings in Western Baghdad

or edit of the self's corrupted text:
the prefixed Word against the suffixed.

Your word against mine, and mine against yours.
The Word is never-ending, I suppose –

antidisestablishmentarianism
a curt phoneme in the lexis of Islam –

nor yet begun. So then, it's all bad faith,
as vital to the narrative as death

to life; the picture of a meaning.
The morning moon is yet the evening

moon; zenith is nadir.
Shocked, she remembers yesterday's idea.

Concluding then: in a manner abrupt
and brutal as a rhyming couplet.

5: SYRIA

A novelist in horror of an ending
resolves to write an alternate beginning,

make history a ramified version
of itself, a road-to-Damascus vision

as seen by (the old sectarian) Saul
of Tarsus, a future written by St Paul.

Bored of all this by now, her systematics
break down like supply-lines to Damascus –

date trees, wells, the enchanted Qur'an,
Nur al-Din Ali and Bar al-Din Hasan,

tall tales told as civic destiny
blood, oil, and sand. Foreign policy

rewritten as myth: *Barack Obama's*
'don't do stupid stuff' put paid to Homs,

Aleppo, all the citizens thereby.
Her characters can't go to Araby

to spend their ha'p'orth at the old bazaar;
BBC News and Al-Jazeera

outspend them there with gilt-edged fiction
(fact plus fiction equals faction).

Deletes the lot, by way of denouement,
being both a devil and a woman,

Allahu-akbar. Her central character
returns into what's known as 'the aether'.

August 2014

TO THE CHOIR

the rage of Caliban seeing his own face in a glass

'The *bigotry* that dare not speak its name...'
Not a bad first line, if a wee bit gauche,
appropriating Wildean farouche,
the author, one trusts, spinning off the norm.

Instead of bigotry, shouldn't it be *love*?
It's about political correctness!
Evoking that angel-in-the-wilderness
rhetoric of injured merit. Interesting enough –

putting Wilde in the wilderness, art in thou art.
Ha ha, very good. So... is that it?

No. Thou art 'corrupt without being charming,
finding ugly meanings in beautiful things'.

Plus, to be clear, it isn't jealousy
that drives this poem, but your outrageous
ostracisms; it is an elegy,
not for your endlessly coprophagous

human circle, feeding meme by meme,
but for a bigotry that dare not speak its name.

...

Your lives are not your own – or anyone's
in fact – but subject to terms and conditions
(prison terms, appalling conditions).
We appeal, distantly, to one another.

Across the ice lake of our common ground,
you range. Pother. Axes being ground,
sparks fly. Social networking was common
in our ancestors; you are no exception.

There's something primitive about all this.
You do not know that you are primitive.
To come to terms, acknowledge your conditions.
I say again, your lives are not your own.

...

Hmm. Leaving all that poetry aside,
let's analyse your self-styled 'edginess'.
Like protozoa of a common genus
it's less an edge, I think, and more a side

you're on, at best; at worst, the circumference
of a petri dish, a purulent gunk.
The specimens of human effluence
show up, in UV lighting, sprays of pink.

Long live your microscopic culture!
Caliban, the dog, had dignity,
knowing himself to be a bastard creature,
his loneliness a bright, fantastic city.

...

Making metaphors of you may be construed
as violence translated into language,
or, worse, hauteur, born of some privilege
to banish the accused before she's tried.

Privilege is private law. I do to
you what you have done, summarily, to her.
And there it is, shouted from the back: 'to err
is human, to forgive, divine.' True, true...

But we are Phaemon's dogs, make metaphor
of ourselves to scrap for scraps of swine,
the fangs, the meat, the bones, the pink saliva,
being neither human nor divine.

That's the way it is. No reason to be bitter.
Embrace the backside of yourself, and kiss it better.

...

Fudging your reflections, those cack-handed smears –
Calibans rejigging in a hall of mirrors.

THE REAL

1
Back of the field, encircled
by a fence and then
a ring of trees,
the old school pond –

forbidden ground,
essayed by no-one ever
on pain of expulsion;
studiously ignored, as though

to enter in
the precinct of that fence
was a tribe's transgression,
ritual and taboo.

Miraculous to tell.
On good authority,
by instinct,
these being much the same,

we'd had it;
even to think it
appalling as the crime
of shattering windows.

2

As with the bomb-shelter
near the old prefabs,
squat as a kiln;
boarded up

but for a slot through which
on tiptoe you could
have a squint:
darkness, rubble, filigrees

of great black cobwebs;
the schoolboy's
anti-charm and totem,
glimpsed with the dawning gloom

of ancient nudity,
like antlers,
genitalia.
Do not enter.

3

The house of your dreams
has no door. But
hidden: there may be a trap,
tight-lipped, shut mouth

of a tunnel,
leading to... Leading to...
By nature hidden
behind the mythos of its trees

the pond, forbidden and forbidding
(whirlpool, black hole, grave-pit).
On good authority
it was a pond all right

but none approached it,
not one of us approached the fence.
It could have been anything.
It could have been anything at all.

4
That stylised, universal
cock and balls —
unmentionables
squinnied at through the dark;

the unspeakable,
too powerful for words,
it fades over time,
crumbling with the brick

but visible
for generations,
stark as a retinal flash.
(And in a bomb-shelter too;

there's symbolism.)
A charm to appease the gods
of what-we-won't-mention,
to quiet

not summon them,
as we had thought;
and the Law an emanation
of that silence.

5
Not looking at it
made it powerful.
Looking at it
made it seem powerful.

Wind worries at it.
Perspectives wrap around
it. Silence
warps like a wave

oscillating in
to the event horizon,
the dead centre
of the real

6
An epic of conspiratorial proportions.
The pond was real, still is −
that is, was nothing
particularly special:

tawny, concave water,
a housing estate,
unresponsive
but for the occasional desperate slap

of sun. Trees and fences,
tall grass, footballs
immemorial as toadstools
wheezing their last

was what it was, or was it...
Unrepeatable terrain;
up to my eyes
in mud, blood, bodies.

KNOWLEDGE

Nobody likes a smartarse.

Let it be said

I know this, and I know it knowingly.

Now when I say I know it knowingly I mean
I know it for what it is,
self-evident as the self's evidence of itself,
true as truism —

self-fulfilling as a repeated phrase,
repeated as a self-fulfilling phrase.

Childhood's knowledge isn't knowing knowledge.
Childhood doesn't teach you this. It can't.

Teachers teach
the facts of life and not the fact of life
that nobody likes a smartarse.

Take this as direct unadorned instruction.

Repeat it after me.

Memorise it,
or write it down,
you idiot.

Nobody likes a smartarse.
Nobody likes a smartarse.
Nobody likes a smartarse.

BODY AND SOUL

I walked into my heaven gingerly
as an office junior walks into a meeting late:
making great show of not making a show
I crept in, histrionically pious,
pulled out a chair, sat down
as though it were of superheated iron.
Where've you been? the chairman jabbed toward me,
smiling. I got my notebook out
and sat, without a pen,
once more a functioning cell in the corporate body.

I walked into the boardroom gingerly
as Adam back into the Garden of Eden
(Eve will join us later on a video call from London)
creeping, exaggeratedly careful
not to fall
and eased a chair out as though it were a mandrake root.
We know where you've been, intoned
the supersensible heavenly host.
It's tough out there in the current climate, we know.
The overhead fluorescent light
pulsated gently to my reanimated spirit.

IRISH DANCING

You've been through mental illness,
burned it off
like a dancer's callus
making the dancer callous
to her bouncing, shivering, wooden floor,
or with every planted step she feels it more.
In pounding it the skin grows tough.

Or as the ear with shrillness,
slowly deaf.
Though the dancer performs
unimpeachable pavanes
she can't feel her feet are killing her
or – though the music's all the way up – hear
the beat she treads, how sharp, how rough.

The dancer's deafness,
the dancer's toughness:
a way of moving, an inurement
to constraining that is itself constraint.
But now your skin's sore
you feel every floor

make feíle and feís
of sensitive flesh,
quake in the thunderous argument
of new-born earth and consummate infant,
and reel, spin, and soar
beyond metaphor.

APOLOGY

The real artist is a clumsy one.

Meaning?
Meaning

For the clumsy expression
of frustration and frustration
of expression
being
one and the same
two sides of a wobbling, pirouetting coin

they are their world
the flinch of gravity

flailing; pure
Newtonian slapstick.

Boredom's the same,
or something like it.

Experience the experience of experience.

Kerfuffle.
What?

And honest people know themselves
dishonest.

3

SECULAR GAMES

Experience consists in experiencing what we do not wish to
experience.

— Sigmund Freud, *Jokes and their Relation to the Unconscious*

1

Reading Freud's book on joke-technique
I hear an advert for the latest Audi
on the TV – *Vorsprung durch Technik* –
followed by the weather. A cold front, cloudy.
Expect the tick-tock-tick-tock
of drizzle any second now. Get ready.

Get set, for the endless race of traffic
to drown out in the wash... The mobile purrs
with messages, news, garishly graphic
as a post-traumatic toddler's crayon pictures.
There is a horror which is unhorrific
and, as they say, it never rains but pours.

I found a thing about experience –
how people keep on coming back like addicts,
despite the obvious appearance
of reality, for a bad fix,
eunuch masochists, like T.E. Lawrence,
collect experiences like products.

Freud doesn't actually say it like that,
of course. I've just seen *Lawrence of Arabia*.
Embarrassing as Yasser Arafat,
messianic, the anti-Dubya,
he wanted paradise by holy fiat,
lost his mind instead; mistook his Saviour

for himself, out in the wrong desert;
tempted by a white, male, British Satan
to make of immortality a dead cert:
the ghost of Charles George Gordon in Sudan;
a pillar of fire, a cloud of dust and dirt
leading him on through picturesque Jordan.

Like Lawrence, I want my mastery
to be adored, as a reluctant man
conscripted into public history.
The sword, indeed, is mightier than the pen.
Humility is often vanity,
the human in the mask of the humane.

Nowadays a writer can't dictate...
What's all this got to do with Sigmund Freud?
Not much, perhaps... nor the Audi advert.
You may be disappointed, I'm afraid,
but please do not indict what I indite.
There is no peace among a people freed –

by which I mean, the illusion of freedom
should be maintained as such, though freedom's real;
though I suspect that what we call our doom
is, in fact, what we also call free will
and, like art, we become ourselves through form
(without the right to speak for other people).

2

Communicant, at television's altar,
my point of view becomes reality's.
Drizzle's metronomic pitter-patter
titivates the quivering ears of trees,
I can imagine, in the grey-blue yonder.
Heaney wrote about Diogenes

who searched for one just man and was a cynic:
you may as well sit back and watch TV.
Or, better yet, drink up that arsenic,
watch the living room go topsy-turvy
and the walls collapse away into the scenic
pastoral heaven of the Teletubby.

Or say to yourself, *I'm feeling fairly Zen*,
making a Void of the sucking bullet-wound.
Obscenities; the whitewashed walls of Hebron;
the bony plains of 'war-torn' Helmand
Province. Such images thrum in the brain,
the brain that may or may not be a mind –

the brain that may or may not be a dynamo –
pulsing like aleph in its jar of bone.
Picture that: the very substance of the animal
settled in its pickling-jar of brine.
I tell you what, if brains were dynamite…
If Mr Scarecrow only had a brain…

So, if a picture tells a thousand stories,
do we then develop into pictures?
The ancients knew it: *ut pictura poeisis*
in the *Ars Poetica* of Horace.
(Devil's advocate, you may cite poetry's
metamorphosing of lyres into liars.)

Beats obsessing over this word, that word,
like Hamlet gibbering at Polonius:
Words words words… Do you not know me, my Lord?
Ay sir, to be honest, as this world goes…
To be honest is to be like a god
in apprehension; to rise up into madness.

3
Behold the day. It could be Christ's chrism
effervescing down the pub's front steps,
ethereal spume, archangel's jism;
glister-gold streamlets coming to their stops
at storm-drains and the gutter. Ectoplasm.
Foam-slushy water from the cellar's taps.

A single line of scripture sparked a sermon
in the olden days; something on conscience;
or more medieval, obscure, like simony,
say, even weirder than *Corinthians* –
prayers for the grubbing soul of Simon –
the congregation huge, awesome with patience.

Your silver perish with you, for God's gift
is not available at any price
(you've reached the limit of your overdraft).
Precision-engined music of the diss,
like the Augustans: like Jonathan Swift
(whose style may be better served in prose)

for whom God's gift was God-given gumption –
common sense, that is – and the golden mean,
good writing as the low road of redemption
provided it's produced by self-loathing men.

Women occasionally get a mention.
You have to soil yourself to be made clean.

Take little popinjay Christopher Smart
who died of fever in a debtors' jail:
washed, at the last, in the black blood of his art —
Jubilate Agno on the madhouse wall —
or victim of malfeasance and of tort,
locked up by his friends, harrowed into hell?

I don't know where I'm going, I confess —
but neither do you. Why should I speak differently.
I warned you about buying into this.
Jesus' footprints on the Sea of Galilee
are tracks across a paper-thin veneer of ice,
the visionary saints had epilepsy.

You may well think yourself more pricks than kicks
but you would make the world your testament
like desert fathers risen into bishoprics
or risen into bliss, the hill of Stormont.
It is hard for thee to kick against the pricks.
Scratch that motto to your moral torment.

4

Well, that was nice — and here we go again.
The rain is tap-tap-tapping at the window,
a water-spirit wanting to come in.
The game is on. Get ready — get set — go
crazy while you still warrant some attention.
Do a watercolour of a rainbow

large as life, at 1:1 scale;
make Silent Valley reservoir your canvas
propped up on the cityscape your easel.
The acoustic qualities of caverns
speak for themselves; be your own singing school,
more Eurydice than Orpheus:

whose name means 'justice far and wide'
was lost to subterranean deities
while he tripped onward in the sunlight world
widdling his oracular ditties
(Zeus appears, occasionally, on a cloud
of thunder, of ambiguous divinities).

Perhaps Eurydice went on a bit
so, making the right noises, he looked back,
carrying on then with his lifelong habit
of self-involution. Not a bad trick –
she disappearing like a startled rabbit,
he letting love be the food of music.

Torn apart by Maenads at last, of course,
as a symbol of poetic justice
or the vengeance of women; or of Zeus,
cameo-maker, actor of atrocities
and of violent, arbitrary grace,
thunder his applause-track, a handpicked audience.

Droplets, constellations, on the glass gather,
glowing sun-pocks, a random pattern
of galaxies transparently throughother;
dimpled the clear skin of the sky-tarn.
Tell me all about your vengeful father
through interpretive dance. Take a funny turn.

Or write an endless poem in a form
recalling Auden, maybe Yeats, Muldoon,
but not as good. Yes, like this poem –
sign of a good meal – better out than in.
Email it to somebody back home
who'll say he likes it, but what does it mean?

5
Secular games. The worldly festival
put on by populising emperors
to sell themselves to history – civil
ordinance, metaphysical prowess –
the kind of thing described by Juvenal
in Satire Ten as bread and circuses.

The kinds of things described by Robert Graves
in the Claudius books (infuriate
the god of history). Virgil's bee-hives
emblematic of the Roman state.
I'll leave him with you. Make sure he behaves.
Caligula half-inched his father's Hecate.

Roll up – roll up – for uncredited posterity.
The grand unveiling; curtains whisked away
revealing, not Juno, the goddess Astarte
mother of fertility and war
from Carthage. The age of austerity.
Bloody foreigners coming over here.

With her pecks and bushels and her chariot
acting like she owns the fucking place,
arse-backwards to the proletariat –

a foreign goddess in the Field of Mars!
Return the fasces for the lariat!
Just to be clear, my own mother's Maltese.

I don't know what the hell I'm talking about.
Behind the curtain is another curtain
and behind that... behind that... I tell it straight:
the expectation of a gift, a guerdon
of the gods, will lifelong be frustrate,
empty-handedness the only thing that's certain.

Expectation that has come to nothing –
Immanuel Kant's definition of comedy.
That being so, why is no one laughing?
It's your condescending manner, comrade.
Bring in the plebs, their effing and jeffing,
hilarity and camaraderie,

the grumbling underbelly of the games.
Wash down those fish-heads with Salerian wine.
Let them eat their barley and legumes!
Caligula was killed in public, alone,
imperious among imperiums.
For Christ's sake turn that bloody racket down.

I feel the pointed drippings of anxiety;
the windowpane with drizzle pitter-patters.
Impossible to write this, to Do My Duty
and finish well, like Roman senators,
the soul discharged, winnowing back to Blighty.
At least, in the end, none of this much matters.

6

Psychogeography – discuss. Place-names
of Britain like little Freudian slips
belying ancient meaning: pseudonyms
that underwrite the Ordinance Survey maps,
genius loci swapped for garden gnomes,
buckwheat interfering with the buttercups,

grey squirrels pillaging the blackberries
and the land lilting madly: *halgh* and *hough*,
thorpe, *gate*, lying dormant on the barrows
while on the tasteless tongue lies that *broagh*
the English mutilate, abuse, embarrass –
the muffle filter on the seismograph.

Yes, that's a certain kind of narrative,
in which the culture with its golden hoard
lies sleeping in its lightly-covered grave
but fitfully, woken by the proper word
which is, of course, natural, descriptive.
Elegy Written in a Country Churchyard –

'Hands that the rod of empire might have swayed,
Or waked to ecstasy the living lyre'
and all the rest of it. The glebe and sward;
chemical outflow in the River Wyre;
silence being mightier than the sword,
the dead lamenting, meekly, their messiah;

poems like little parcels of sugar
your tongue cracks open, and there's nothing inside;
no chocolate melting, thickly, from the centre;
brittle confectionery of the void
at its own heart; and each consumer
whispers sweet nothings inside his own head.

Better nothing than this oozy bitterness
contaminating the river-water
that feeds the hundred of Amounderness.
What will they think. Owd Lancashire
voices cry terror against the witches.
Look it up on Wikipedia –

the testimony of Grace Sowerbutts,
the examination of James Device –
and seek no further for the British state's
demonisation of its underclass.
A pox o' magistrates and feffnicutes
(the beggar and the Justice of the Peace)

So odious unto all their neighbours
and so feared… Another desolated culture.
Malkin Tower's fine upstanding doors
nailed on, all else gone back to nature,
tumbledowns of photogenic colours.
Read the numen into nomenclature.

Adverts for imaginary products.
Come and join your local witches' sabbat –
it'll work a charm! Pacify heretics
through advertising; permissively prohibit
the heresy of the autodidacts.
Malkin Tower is The Palace of Shit.

7
Unaccustomed as I am to public speaking
let there be light – or, if that's not possible,
let there be… Well, let there be… something.
Maybe translate the *New International Bible*

into Maltese, or try – now you're talking! –
something equally unconscionable.

Write about what you know. The bloody cheek
of it – if only I *could* know what I knew.
Christianity is mistranslated Greek
which itself is mistranslated Hebrew
the Pharisees and scribes could barely speak.
Purblindness ratifies your purview.

What's with the metric, mate? Rudyard Kipling
had the insight to go imperial...
Saying nothing, one yet says everything.
That's all very well.... That's all very... well.
Yet you, my poorly reader, sit there, reading,
gently, for richer, for poorer, good or ill.

See the Church of England wedding service,
broad fosses of silver-watery light
glazing the imperfections of the novice,
glittering the dress; the bride arriving late –
five hundred years late – for *ora pro nobis*,
the poshness of otherworldly Latin.

FIAT LUX. That reminds me of the Audi,
that optimistic *Vorsprung durch Technik* –
progress through technology – the body
beautiful as the body politic –
and the turning weather. A cold front, cloudy;
drizzle's tick-tock-tick-tock.

But no, I must resist the timely circle.
Truth be told, I began this poem in March;
it's now April; the seasonal cycle

won't do as symbol; nor will *Vorsprung durch
Technik*. As spring commemorates the icicle
by melting it, so will my closing speech

evoke the icicle's liquidity,
metastability, dissipation
the name of the game. Remember? TV
parodies permanent revolution
with revolting permanence; gravity
unquantifiable in quantum.

I still don't know, and now I never will,
what on earth all this was leading to.
The secular games were ritual renewal,
sacrificial death, goodbye and hello –
an art that is accessible to all.
Take your places. Get ready. Get set. Go.

NOTES

'Italy'
The poem refers to Carlo Borromeo (1538-1584), Archbishop of Milan.

'Four Versions of Borges'
The epigraph is taken from the preface to Borges's book of poems *La Cifra*, or *The Limit*, and means 'to give and to receive is the same thing'.

'The Isle of Man'
'As likely Wonderland as Newfoundland, | America.'
The sense of this is 'Newfoundland, *or* America.'

'The Silkworm Chamber'
Sima Qian, author of the work known in the West as *Records of the Grand Historian*, neglected, or refused, to condemn a general who failed to defeat the emperor's enemy in battle. Given the choice of death or castration, Sima Qian chose the latter, so that he might continue and finish his history.

ACKNOWLEDGEMENTS

Some of these poems have previously appeared in *PN Review*, *Stand*, *Ulster Tatler*, *Glasgow Review of Books*, *Poetry Proper*, *The Yellow Nib*, *New Poetries V* (Carcanet), *Incertus* (Netherlea), and *Landing Places: Immigrant Poets in Ireland* (Dedalus).

I gratefully acknowledge financial support from the Arts Council of Northern Ireland towards the completion of this book.

TITLES INCLUDE